Feed Me!

Simon Tofield

CANONGATE

Edinburgh-London-New York-Melbourne

To Jo Euston-Moore and Sarah Alexander

Published by Canongate Books in 2011

1

Simon's Cat (2009) and Simon's Cat: Beyond the Fence (2010)
were first published in Great Britain by Canongate Books Ltd,
14 High Street, Edinburgh EH1 1TE

www.canongate.tv

Colouring and layout by Stuart Polson

British Library Cataloguing-in-Publication Data
A catalogue record for this book is available on
request from the British Library

ISBN 978 0 85786 277 8

Printed and bound in Italy by Grafica Veneta S.p.A.

CRUNCH
CA

MENU

For all your Simon's Cat goodies, check out the webshop at

www.simonscat.com